CLAUDIA SAID SÍ!

The Story of México's First Woman President

BY **DEBORAH BODIN COHEN** AND **KERRY OLITZKY**

ILLUSTRATED BY **CARLOS VELEZ AGUILERA**

For my brother-in-law Bruce Cohen
who, like Claudia, believes in science. — D.B.C.

To honor the memory
of Rabbi David J. Susskind. — K.O.

To my dear mother, Consuelo — C.V.A.

Editorial consultation by Dr. Tessy Schlosser, political theorist and historian, Director General of The Mexican Jewish Documentation and Research Center CDIJUM

Apples & Honey Press
An Imprint of Behrman House Publishers
Millburn, New Jersey 07041
www.applesandhoneypress.com

ISBN 978-1-68115-713-9

Text copyright © 2025 by Kerry Olitzky and Deborah Bodin Cohen
Illustrations copyright © 2025 by Behrman House

Photograph of Claudia Sheinbaum: Wikimedia/EneasMx

All rights reserved. No part of this publication may be translated, reproduced, stored in a retrieval system or transmitted, in any form or by any means, electronic, mechanical, photocopying, recording or otherwise, for any purpose, without express written permission from the publishers.

Library of Congress Cataloging-in-Publication Data

Names: Cohen, Deborah Bodin, 1968- author. | Olitzky, Kerry M., author. | Vélez, Carlos, 1980- illustrator.
Title: Claudia said sí! : the story of Mexico's first woman president / by Deborah Bodin Cohen and Kerry Olitzky ; illustrated by Carlos Vélez Aguilera.
Other titles: Story of Mexico's first woman president
Description: Millburn, New Jersey : Apples & Honey Press, an imprint of Behrman House Publishers, [2025] | Audience: Ages 4-8 | Audience: Grades 2-3 | Summary: "Meet Mexico's first woman president. From social justice activist to Nobel-winning scientist to the first woman as well as the first Jewish president of Mexico, Claudia Sheinbaum faces each new challenge by saying, "sí!", "yes, I can.""-- Provided by publisher.
Identifiers: LCCN 2024052513 | ISBN 9781681157139 (hardcover)
Subjects: LCSH: Sheinbaum Pardo, Claudia--Juvenile literature. | Women presidents--Mexico--Biography--Juvenile literature. | Presidents--Mexico--Biography--Juvenile literature. | Jewish women--Mexico--Biography--Juvenile literature. | Jews--Mexico--Biography--Juvenile literature. | Women scientists--Mexico--Biography--Juvenile literature. | Scientists--Mexico--Biography--Juvenile literature. | Mexico City (Mexico)--Biography--Juvenile literature.
Classification: LCC F1236.9.S54 C64 2025 | DDC 972.08/44092 [B]--dc23/eng/20250102
LC record available at https://lccn.loc.gov/2024052513

Design and art direction by Zach Marell
Edited by Dena Neusner
Printed in China

9 8 7 6 5 4 3 2 1

When Claudia Sheinbaum was a child, millions of *mariposas* would visit México each autumn. Most of the butterflies settled in the mountains, blanketing fir trees like copper silk.

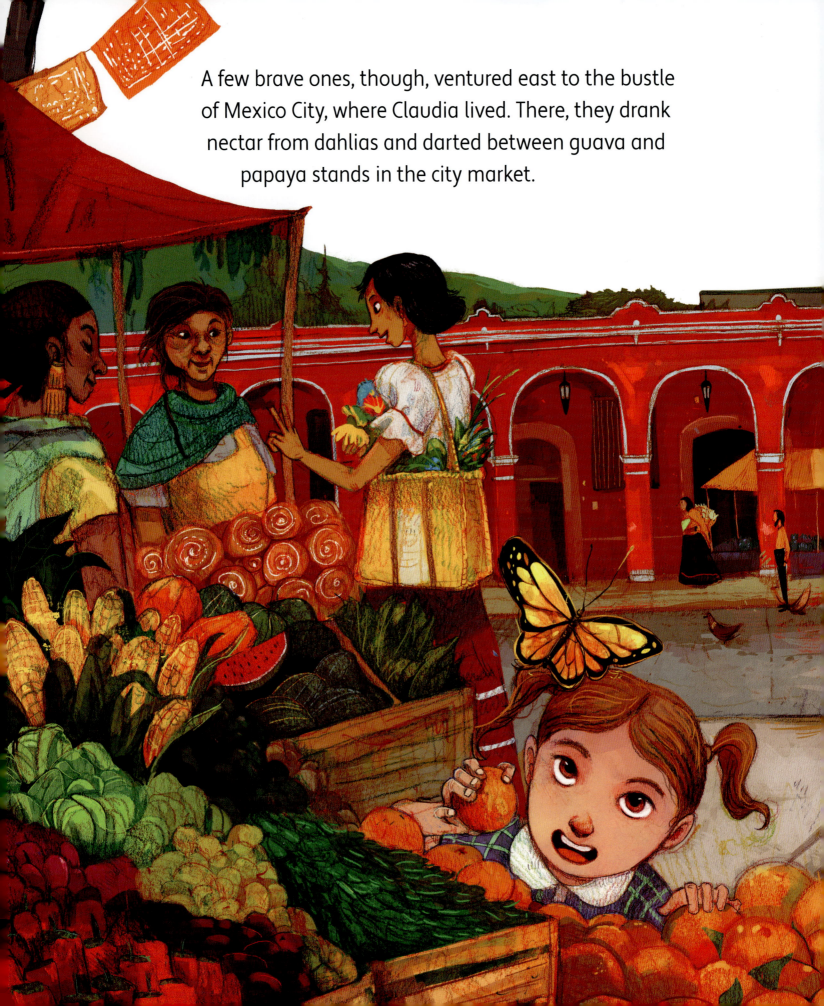

A few brave ones, though, ventured east to the bustle of Mexico City, where Claudia lived. There, they drank nectar from dahlias and darted between guava and papaya stands in the city market.

When the mariposas arrived, Claudia knew the festival of Hanukkah wasn't far behind. Claudia lit the Hanukkah *menorá* with her grandparents, her *abuelo* and *abuela*. They laughed and sang Jewish holiday songs as the candles burned.

Outside, the mariposas danced like flames in the wind.

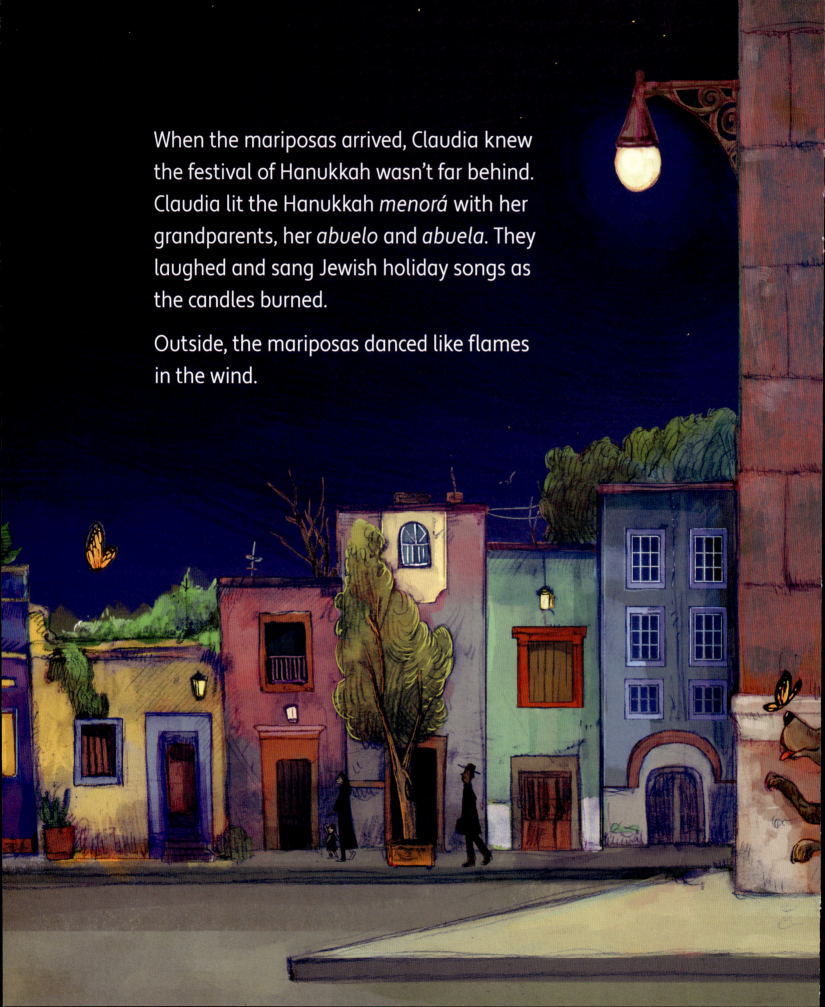

At school, Claudia's teacher taught the life cycle of the mariposa. "The caterpillar forms a jade-green shell called a *chrysalis* and tucks itself inside.

There, it experiences a *metamorphosis*, an amazing transformation.

After weeks of growth and change,
the chrysalis cracks open and a mariposa emerges."

Me•ta•mor•pho•sis. Five syllables. Was it the
longest word that Claudia knew?

As time passed, Claudia grew and changed, too. The schoolgirl who loved nature grew into a teenage ballerina who rehearsed until her muscles ached,

who then changed into an outspoken activist, leading rallies for fair government and free education for all.

What didn't change? Claudia's persistence.

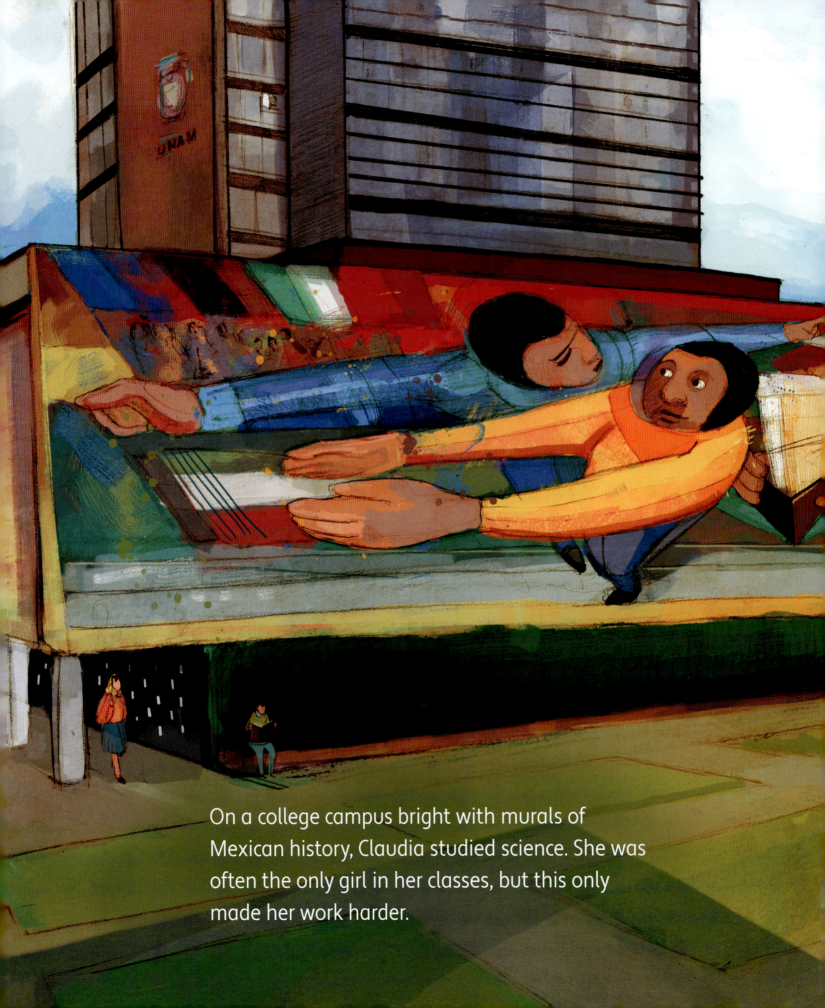

On a college campus bright with murals of Mexican history, Claudia studied science. She was often the only girl in her classes, but this only made her work harder.

Claudia studied year after year. She earned degree after degree. Then one day, her own chrysalis cracked open, and Dr. Claudia Sheinbaum emerged, an expert on the environment.

Behind an office door that now read "Profesora Sheinbaum," Claudia researched and wrote reports about air, water, and land that had become dirty with trash and chemicals.

She studied the problems, made her best guesses about how to solve them, and then tested her guesses.

Could using electric vehicles reduce pollution? How about solar power or windmills? What if there were better buses and trains, so there could be fewer cars on the roads?

When not in her office, Claudia biked through city parks with her children or tended to her garden.

But with each passing year, the air smelled more and more like smog—from factories, construction, and cars. And there was less rain, which made gardening more difficult.

Even the mariposas were suffering. Each year, fewer of them fluttered through the sky. Soon, would there be any left?

Claudia thought, *I want to do more. I want to put my research into action.*

Mexico City's new mayor heard about Claudia's research.

He asked, "I want less pollution in our city. Do you know how to do that?"

"Sí," answered Claudia humbly. "If I have a team to help me."

So the mayor asked, "Would you be Mexico City's Secretary of the Environment?"

This time, Claudia didn't need to think hard or study the options. She grinned. "Sí!"

The team talked and debated, analyzed and dreamed.

Problem: The air is dirty and unhealthy to breathe.

Solution: Plant trees to clean the air, millions and millions of them.

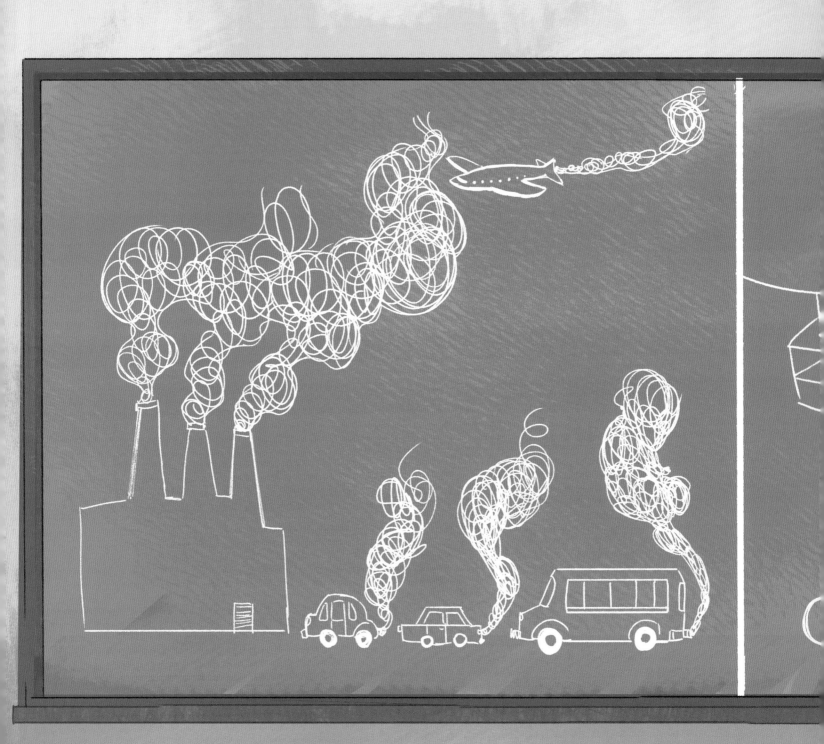

Problem: There's too much traffic, causing pollution.

Solution: Provide more buses instead of cars. Offer free bicycles. Promote electric cars.

Some of their solutions worked, and some did not. When they did not work, Claudia and her team tried again.

Around the world, scientists heard about Claudia's changes in Mexico City. The United Nations sent an invitation. Would she like to join an international team studying climate change? Sí!

Soon, Claudia was sharing ideas with scientists from Australia to Zambia—and nearly 100 countries in between. When the Nobel Peace Prize was announced, the international team had won it!

The people of Mexico City saw all the changes around them. They heard about the Nobel Prize. They called Claudia "La Doctora"—a sign of respect.

They voted for Claudia to be their mayor.

She got to work with her team right away.

Could she create electric power without more pollution? Sí!

Claudia saw that Mexico City had plenty of sunshine, which made it perfect for solar energy. When the sun shines onto a solar panel, the panel converts the sun's energy into electricity.

But in such a crowded city, where could they put the solar panels? Central de Abasto, one of the largest public markets in the world, had an enormous flat roof. *Perfecto*.

Could she help people get good jobs? Sí!

Claudia knew that many poorer people lived high up in the hills. It took hours on buses to get to the city center, where there were good jobs. How could the city help?

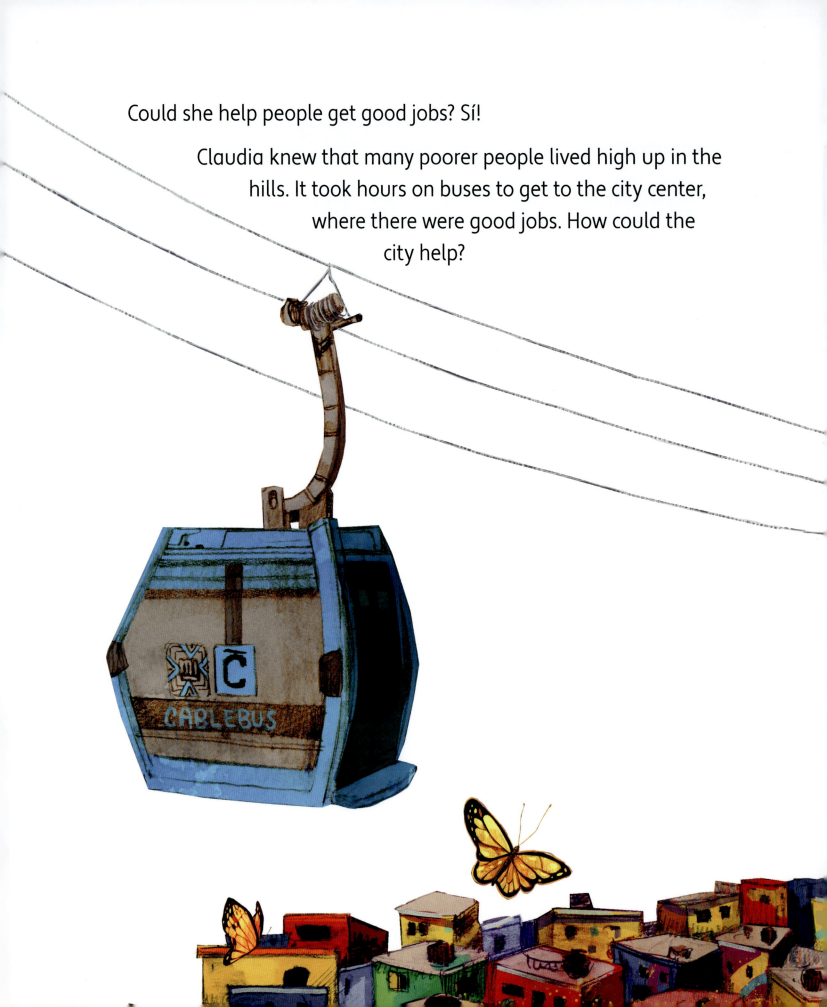

Claudia glanced toward the sky where eagles soared.

In Colombia, some people used cable cars to get to work. Maybe the same solution would work in Mexico City.

She and her team installed the Cablebús system, connecting the hills to the city center.

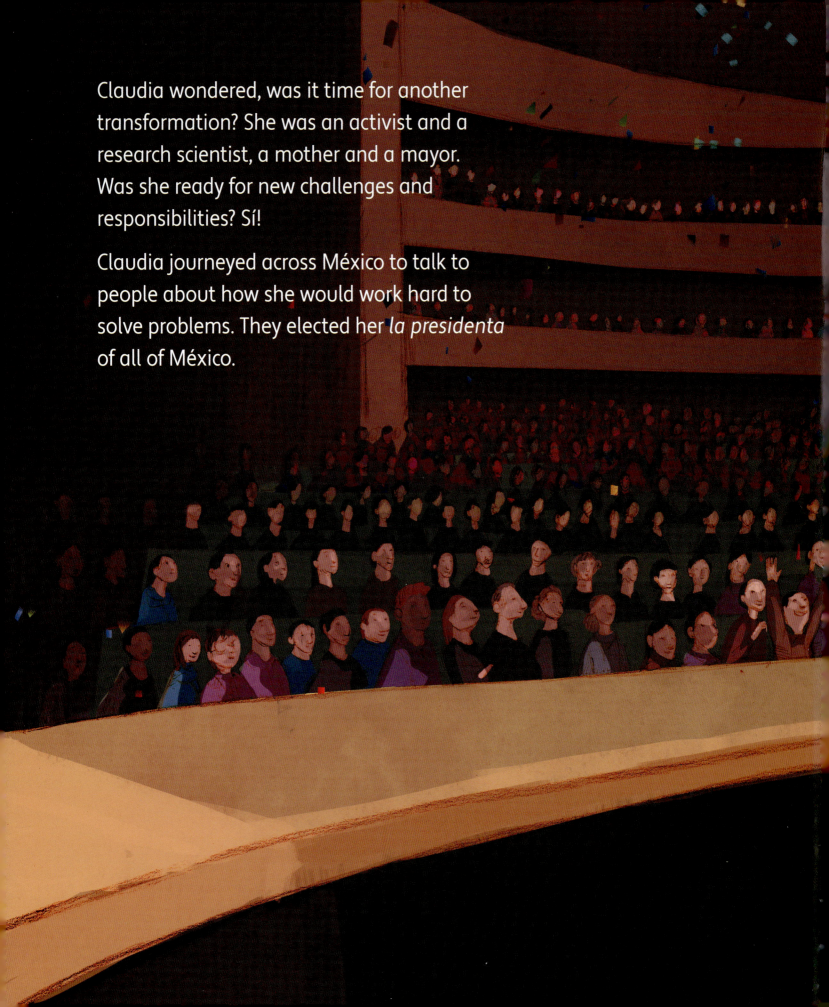

Claudia wondered, was it time for another transformation? She was an activist and a research scientist, a mother and a mayor. Was she ready for new challenges and responsibilities? Sí!

Claudia journeyed across México to talk to people about how she would work hard to solve problems. They elected her *la presidenta* of all of México.

Claudia glanced toward the sky where eagles soared.

In Colombia, some people used cable cars to get to work. Maybe the same solution would work in Mexico City.

She and her team installed the Cablebús system, connecting the hills to the city center.

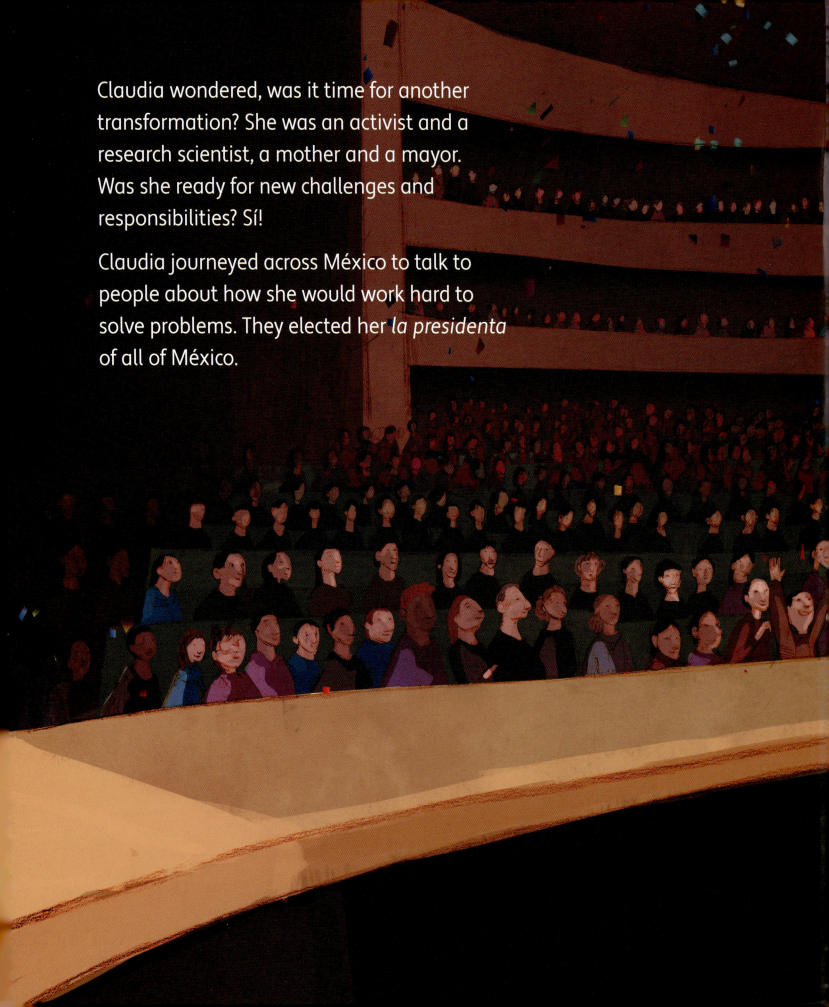

Claudia wondered, was it time for another transformation? She was an activist and a research scientist, a mother and a mayor. Was she ready for new challenges and responsibilities? Sí!

Claudia journeyed across México to talk to people about how she would work hard to solve problems. They elected her *la presidenta* of all of México.

She was the first woman, the first Jewish person, and the first scientist to lead the country.

A metamorphosis indeed.

Dear Readers,

Like a caterpillar changing into a butterfly, every person experiences transformations in their lifetime. Claudia Sheinbaum did, and so will you!

Who have you been? Who do you hope to become? A scientist? An activist? A prima ballerina? Maybe president? It's a great journey, isn't it?

—Kerry and Debbie

Spanish Words to Know

Abuela: grandmother

Abuelo: grandfather

La Doctora: the doctor

La Presidenta: the president

Mariposa: (plural *mariposas*) butterfly

Menorá: Hanukkah menorah

Perfecto: perfect

Sí: yes

The Jewish Community in México

Today, between 40–60,000 Jews live in México, the majority in Mexico City. The first Jews arrived in México over 500 years ago, fleeing religious persecution in Spain and Portugal. They hoped to find a friendlier home, but, even in México, they had to practice their Judaism secretly. Finally, after México gained its independence from Spain in 1821, the new country allowed more religious freedom. A small, active Mexican Jewish community

prospered. More Jewish immigrants arrived, both Ashkenazi Jews from Eastern Europe and Sephardic Jews from Southern Europe and the Middle East. Claudia Sheinbaum's family represents this diversity. Her parents' families came from Jewish communities in Lithuania and Bulgaria.

As a child, Claudia celebrated the Jewish holiday of Hanukkah with her grandparents. On Hanukkah, Jewish people light candles for eight nights to remember a miracle from long ago, when a small group of people won their freedom from an oppressive king and a tiny amount of oil lasted for eight days.

The Nobel Peace Prize

Every year, our planet grows warmer. In 1988, the United Nations, realizing that countries need to work together to solve this problem, created the Intergovernmental Panel on Climate Change. The panel brought together 600 scientists and lawmakers from around the world to study global warming and develop international solutions—including Claudia Sheinbaum. In 2007, panel members shared the Nobel Peace Prize for working together to build knowledge and awareness about climate change.

Mexican Women Lead

Today, nearly half of México's Congress is female. Mexican women hold top positions in business, science, and public life. But México wasn't always so open to women leaders. In fact, Mexican women were not even allowed to vote in México until 1955.

How did it happen? In the last 20 years, México passed a series of laws to protect women's rights and encourage their leadership. "It is time for women," said Claudia Sheinbaum when she became President of México. "Women have arrived to shape the destiny of our beautiful nation."

Claudia Sheinbaum, October 2024